The Single Woman Hamster Workbook

Volume Three of
The Sit 'N' Do Nothing
Hamster Series

Humans All Make Some Time Exploring Relationships

Written By Wendy Proteau

Covers designed by: Wendy Proteau

The Single Woman Hamster

Why a Hamster? It is that continual engine that keeps spinning the wheel in our minds. We think every moment of every day! Choices, twists, turns, preferences, decisions…every moment of every day we think constantly!

Ever stop to really reflect on who you are, where ya been and what ya want? I'm betting your life is busy and you go through the motions doing what needs to be done. You have hobbies, friends, family, kids and schedules to keep. I'm thinking you've never taken time just to think about it all.

For whatever reason you're holding this book, perhaps a gift from a friend, family member, best friend or a secret admirer who's had their eye on you. Maybe you've picked it up for something to do on your flight or as you curl up in bed at night. These are simple, shoot from the hip questions.

You are an accumulation of every moment up until now. You've lived, laughed, helped, cared and probably touched more lives than you thought. Some questions are things guys want to know and some are things women ponder in life. Men are men and women are women. I wonder if we'll ever really get a handle on each other.

You have several people in your life; best friends (male and female), parents, stepparents, brothers, sisters or co-workers. Even people you see through daily routine. Do you talk about all the little things you've done?

With the world moving so fast with internet, text, bills, responsibilities etc…would you recognize a new opportunity if it was at your door or are you so busy that you've missed a few along the way?

Let's just stop for a moment and reflect on it all with just one rule

"GOTTA BE HONEST!"

So grab a pencil, curl up with a blanket and just begin….Enjoy!

Single Female Hamster Basics

Little known facts about_____ and what I think
(First name please)

Today's date:_____

So let's start with the basics of who you are on paper

Last name_____

I live in _____

Born _____ day _____ month _____year

Born in_____

Time I was born was at_____

Raised in_____

Other places I've lived over the years:

_____

_____

_____

Education level is _____

I went to the following schools-name and year please:

_____

_____

_____

I work as a_____

I have been at my current job _____years

I have worked in my trade _____ years

This book was given to me by_____

In 5 words I would describe who I am as

1_____

2_____

3_____

4_____

5_____

In 5 words I would describe the person who gave me this book as

1_____

2_____

3_____

4_____

5_____

See, not so hard is it.....
SO LET'S START HAVING SOME FUN

THE SINGLE WOMAN HAMSTER
Volume three

1-Well here you are, let's see what you're all about. What traits do you think you possess? Now you can't be them all, so only pick the one's that apply to you…on a scale from (1-being totally you (everyone you know would agree), and 10 being not me-rate the one's define you:

____Honest	____Charming
____Independent	____Funny
____Laid back	____Open book
____Stubborn	____Strait forward
____Strong values	____Hard-working
____Bad tempered	____Mouthy
____Passionate	____Sensual
____Loyal	____Strong work ethic
____Shy	____Mysterious
____Strong willed	____Intelligent
____Smart ass	____Coy
____Lazy	____Sexy
____Flirty	____Quiet
____Introvert	____Extrovert
____Creative	____Artistic
____Heart on your sleeve	____Hard to understand
____Loner	____Party girl

2-That wasn't so hard, was it? With these you're one or the other. Some you may relate to both, but you can only pick one or the other on each line. Which one is more honest

Book smart_____   street smart_____

Popular_____   a bit more shy_____

Girly girl_____   don't fuss n bother_____

Dreamer_____   or a realist_____

Woman of her word_____   you maneuver to get your way_____

Aggressive_____   passive_____

Know what you want_____   you'll figure it out as you go_____

Romantic at heart_____   not into all that stuff_____

Dressy/classy_____   casual/relaxed_____

Need attention_____   I'm good on my own_____

Giver_____   taker_____

3-What do you think men would say your best physical features are? Go by the number of compliments you've received on each…rate each of these, (#1 is for my best feature to #12 for not my best)

Hair_____   stomach_____   legs_____

Eyes_____   teeth/smile _____   bum_____

Smile_____   arms _____   feet_____

Chest_____   cheekbones _____   calves_____

4-At times, we are our own worst critics and we all have something we wish we could change. What one thing would you like to change from the above list? Remember its only one,-gotta keep the rest!

Change: _____

Change it to be more: _____

Why:

_____

5-Thinking back over time, use two words to describe yourself as a person and what your best feature was at the time for each of the following ages. Now depending on your current age, you'll have to think to the future and what you hope will be your best in the coming years.

Age	Two words to describe yourself	Best Feature
16	_____	_____	_____
20	_____	_____	_____
30	_____	_____	_____
40	_____	_____	_____
50	_____	_____	_____
60	_____	_____	_____
70	_____	_____	_____
80	_____	_____	_____
90	_____	_____	_____

6-Now that we have you looking back to those early days, let's think on the fun things from your youth, shall we? There are so many memories, things a girl never forgets. So answer all of the following:

Who was your first crush on _____

Did you ever go out with them _____

Who first had a crush on you _____

Did you like that they did _____

Who was your first date _____

How old were you _____

First kiss was from _____

Who was your first real boyfriend _____

How long did it last_____

First real wow kiss was from _____

7-Now we've covered your early years with the first dating moments and boys in your life, so what about things you did or had way back then? Here are some more firsts:

First toy you ever had was a _____

First car you drove was a _____

First car you owned was a _____ _____

First accident you had was with what car _____

First best friend was _____ _____

First big mistake and you got caught by your parents, was when:

_____

_____

First drink you had you were how old _____

First boy/man you had sex with was _____

Where were you when it happened _____

8-So many firsts, now let's think on the overall picture of things. Let's go on the bests so far…no saying you won't have better, just think up until now…

Best vehicle you ever had was _____

Best date you ever had was with _____

Best friend you ever had _____

Best teacher was _____

Best day was when you _____

Best kiss was from _____

Best sex was with _____

Best laugh was with _____

Best pet you ever had was _____

Best toy you ever had was _____

Best deal shopping was _____ _____

9-With the bests, comes the worst! Yep can't have one without the other, gotta take the good with the bad or we wouldn't know the difference, would we?

Worst vehicle you ever owned _____

Worst date was with _____

Worst teacher was _____

Worst day was when you _____

Worst kiss was from _____

Worst sex was with _____

Worst friend turned out to be _____

Worst pet you ever had _____

Worst toy you ever had _____

10-Whew, we got those out of the way. It's hard to think back on all those things. Some make you chuckle though, don't they? What we're ya thinking back then, huh? While we're reminiscing, if you could run into one of your ex-boyfriends who would you most like to see now face to face and sit and have a conversation with:

Who:_____

Why:

_____

_____

_____

11-Now if you could see one of them but they not see you (kinda a fly on the wall scenario) just to see how their life is now, which one would it be? Remember, they wouldn't know you're checking up on them:

Who: _____

Why:

_____

_____

_____

12-How about we find out more about you and how you think about yourself. Let's see which of these you'd choose to describe who you are. You don't have to own it, just pick the one which you can relate to more because it suits your personality and lifestyle. It's only one in each category though:

A)   Classy sedan _____   Sports car _____   Off-road _____

Motorcycle _____   Beater _____

B)   Fine dining _____   Fast foods _____   Home cooking _____

C)   Wine ____   Beer____   Hard stuff_____   Soda _____   Water_____

D)   TV _____   Music ____   Reading ____   Shopping _____

E)   Action ___   Mystery ___   Drama ____   Romance____   Sci-fi_____

F)   Email_____   Phone call _____   Text _____   In person _____

G)   Quiet ____   Talkative ____   The joker ____   The flirt _____

H)   Day at the spa ____   Evening with friends___   Time alone_____

I)   Make up ____   Natural ____   I try ____   Don't care_____

13-We all love movies, they take us away to places we never thought of and we watch lives we only wish we could live. If you could actually live out any one movie, which one would you like to experience as real life? Think about it, action, love scene, heroism…Which role would you like to live out, what scene would you like to experience the most and why?

Movie: _____

You'd be which character: _____

Scene: _____

Why: _____

_____

14-Speaking on the movie topic, let's say you're a starving actress and in the next two years you have 15 roles in upcoming movies. You don't get to choose your parts or orchestrate how you'd want them to go. You have to do all 14 to pay the rent, but could choose the scenes you have to do in order of your preference. Number the list, #1 is the one you'd do first up to #15 the last one (you can add one if you'd like)

____Saloon girl	____Bar room brawl	____Food fight
____Love scene	____Dare devil jumps	____Action hero
____Porno star	____Martial arts	____Old west
____Knight's n damsels	____Space age	____Murder mystery
____Reality show	____Detective/cop	____:_____

15-We all have fears in life, things we just don't like or have never overcome. For some its heights, spiders and some people even have multiples. Do you have any fears? List them:

_____   _____   _____

_____   _____   _____

16-Here's one more fun one, what are all your favorites? These are all things that people may not know about you. Perhaps you've never stopped to think about them all, but we've all got em!

Color _____

Food _____

Fast food _____

Drink _____

Saying _____

Song _____

Band _____

Song to dance to _____ by _____

Song to sing to _____ by _____

Place to be _____

Sport _____

Past time _____

Way to kill time _____

Friend to spend time with _____

Animal _____

Wild animal _____

Pet _____

Clothing outfit _____

Book _____

Movie _____

Cartoon _____

Disney character _____

Work colleague _____

Store to shop in _____

Travel spot _____

Relative _____

That was quite the list! These things just automatically come to mind with little thinking. We know what we like and what we don't!

17-Do you cook? Some are culinary chefs, while others can boil water fairly well, so let's ask these simple questions:

What is your best dish: _____

What would your friends say it is:_____

What would you cook for a date:

_____

What would you cook for a hot date:

_____

Is there a special dessert you'd prepare _____

You would say on a scale from 1-10, 10 being I am a goddess in the kitchen:

I am a: _____

18-Okay let's get tough again. Being single, we get to ask you things you've thought about when it comes to men. What are the first things that attract you to a possible date? Now these are all things you can see from a distance because you don't know who they are, but you're watching them from across the room or see them on a date site. Rate these in order of importance from 1-10 (#1 being this stands out the most about a man)

Eyes_____   Hair_____

Smile_____   Body_____

Confidence level_____   Way he dresses_____

Way he's acting_____   Chest/shoulders_____

Legs_____   Butt_____

Arms_____   Shoes_____

19-So you spotted him across that room or in a chat room and you're curious…so what's next? Do you approach, if so, how? Let's see your method of operation.

Send a message if online   _____ yes _____ no

Send him a drink if in person   _____ yes _____ no

Try to get him to notice you by smiling   _____ yes _____ no

Direct approach, walk up and say:

_____

Be sexy-bat your eyelashes   _____ yes _____ no

Would you try a pick up line   _____ yes _____ no

What line, have you used: _____

Do you sit and wait for him to approach   _____ yes _____ no

Get a friend to approach for you   _____ yes _____ no

Send a napkin with your number   _____ yes _____ no

Ask the waitress to get him to join you   _____ yes _____ no

Accidentally bump into him   _____ yes _____ no

OR (tell us your own methods)

_____

_____

20- I guess fear of rejection is on both sides. We all get rejected. Do you ever wonder how many you missed out on from being afraid to try? So let's find out why we are so afraid: In your mind, the worst thing that could happen if you approach and he's not interested is:

_____

How many you figure you missed out on by not approaching_____

If you could go back and ask just one from your history that you were afraid to approach

Where were you _____

Did you know his name if yes, what was it_____

His online name if on a site _____

21-Well I admit it's not so easy to approach a perfect stranger, so they now have the world of computer date sites and there are a lot of them. Local, worldwide, preferences, body types, financial status…where to start? How you feel about the world of online?

Would you try one _____yes _____no

Have you tried one _____yes _____no

How many have you tried _____

If yes, did you meet anyone interesting _____yes ___   no

How many men didn't work out _____

How many men were off the wall totally _____

How many men ended up as friends _____

How many men would you have liked to get to know more, but never did _____

How many relationships did you have through a site _____

Best one you ever met-screen name was _____

22-Now being the world of computers-you look at a picture/read a profile, chat online for a bit. When you think about it, it opens you up to more possibilities in the world, not just dating local. For that matter, friends can be attained from all over the world. If you've tried a site and you find a possible partner who you just click with:

How long do you like to talk first online _____ days/months/years

Do you want to meet in person right away _____yes _____ no

Do you prefer talking on the phone _____yes _____ no

How would you like to meet them _____ in a group setting or _____ one on one

Do you meet on neutral ground _____yes _____ no

Get them to come to you _____yes _____no

You go to them _____ yes _____no

How far would you drive to go meet someone _____ miles

Would you consider someone for a different country _____yes _____ no

23-Ahhhh…the dating world! Tis not an easy thing, is it? So let's see how you feel about dating in today's society. Twenty years ago things were different, but tis the new millennium, how do you feel about: (Comment on each)

Men making first contact _____

Women making first contact _____

Women kissing him first _____

Men kissing first _____

24-Well some people are more comfortable when things are done a certain way in the dating world. Things changed from days of old, some are still traditional and some are new thinkers. How do you feel about your dating preferences and ideas?

Old fashioned   yes_____ no _____

Open to new idea's   yes_____ no _____

So for a first date then do you:

Prefer to be the one asking   yes_____ no _____

Prefer to make the plan   yes_____ no _____

Prefer if he makes the plan   yes _____ no _____

Like to just meet at the place   yes _____ no _____

Prefer to pick him up   yes _____ no_____

Like if he pays the full bill   yes _____ no _____

Like to pay your portion   yes _____ no _____

Like to pay the full amount   yes _____ no _____

I guess there is a fine line with the date world. We fought for women's rights and equality, so should we be paying our portion? When it comes to romance, does tradition still weigh into things? (your thoughts)

_____

25-Now we've been on this earth together for thousands of years and we still don't understand each other. What are the top 5 things that men do that just drive you crazy in a bad way? You just don't understand why they all seem to do these things:

1-_____

2-_____

3-_____

4-_____

5-_____

26-Now, put the shoe on the other foot-What five things do you do that just ticks men off or they stand their saying what the? Come on, you know we women have our flaws:

1-_____

2-_____

3-_____

4-_____

5-_____

27-Now that you've thought of the worst, what are the top five things that just make it all worth going through?

1-_____

2-_____

3-_____

4-_____

5-_____

28-If you're single now, you must have a list of things that you value and look for in a partner. We all need that physical attraction so that's the start of it all. But what specifics make us want to hold on to someone? Think about it, besides being attracted physically, what are the traits and personality types you think blend perfectly with your life?

Below are several traits just like the one you filled in about yourself at the beginning. Check off things you feel you want. They are options and some may apply, some will be of no importance to you. Just check off the ones you really value. (Not all will apply since no one person can be all these things.) Be realistic!

____Aggressive	____Mechanically inclined		____Sports minded
____Rebel	____Work ethic	____Stubborn	____Loyal
____Independent	____Thoughtful	____Integrity	____Passionate
____Good hearted	____Intelligence	____Easy going	____Understanding
____Humor	____Strong willed	____Caring	____Family values
____Strong morals	____Religious	____Finance smart	____Honesty
____Background	____Sensual	____Expressive	____Quiet/shy
____Hygiene	____Well dressed	____Confident	____Passive
____Outspoken	____Flirtatious	____Imaginative	____Dreamer
____Realist	____Romantic	____Business smart	____Socially Active
____Laid back	____Wealth	____Tough guy	____Sensitive
____Creative/artistic	____Driven	____One of the boys	____Lazy
____Casual	____Athletic	____Conversationalist	____Silent type
____Mysterious	____Open book	____Neat	____Blue-collar
____White-collar	____Risk taker	____Jealous	____Protective

Well that is a few to think about and we can't have everything, but we definitely know what works best for our lives. Now go back and number them in order of importance to you…#1 being the most valuable etc… Thought you were done, huh? (Yikes! This is hard.)

29-When you think about it, to find the absolute perfect partner it takes a lot of work. Maybe by really looking at what we value, it will help us sort through the men in our life. This should be an easy one…With going through the above list it asked what things we truly wish for, so what are the absolute deal breakers-you just will not tolerate a man who: (top 5 only)

1-_____

2-_____

3-_____

4-_____

5-_____

30-Let's change the subject for a bit. We all have done some crazy things in our life. Things we look back on and shake our head saying…why did I? The craziest thing for you would be when:

_____

_____

Along with that, goes the most fun thing we did, and we still smirk when we think about it today. That would be when you:

_____

_____

So, if given the opportunity to do things, if this was all set up for you, paid for-etc…would you: (Some you may have done and love…some would be a new experience.)

Bungee jump	____yes ____no		Skydive	____yes ____no	
Hot air balloon ride	____yes ____no		Ski downhill	____yes ____no	
Water ski	____yes ____no		Go on a safari	____yes ____no	
Mountain Climb	____yes ____no		Motor cross race	____yes ____no	
Cliff dive	____yes ____no		Drive a race car	____yes ____no	
Horseback ride	____yes ____no		Deep sea diving	____yes ____no	

31-Now thinking along those lines, many things are becoming more and more possible everyday with technology so if it ever became available to you would you:

Take a trip into space _____yes _____no

Dive to the bottom of the ocean in a submarine _____yes _____no

Take a ride in an air force jet _____yes _____no

Add your own: _____

32-Thinking back, we all had a dream when we were growing up. We all thought we would grow up to be a veterinarian, doctor, dentist, policewoman, etc…So think way back…

What did you want to be when young _____

What are you doing now _____

Do you like what you do now _____yes _____no

If you could have any job right now right now, anything at all what would you like to be

_____

What do you think your friends would say you'd be best at_____

33-If you could re-experience any one time in your life over again with a partner from the past, like go back in time to one moment…it may take you a while to figure out each of these moments:

A-If you could re-live it exactly the same all over again-(exactly as it happened)-not changing a thing:

How old would you be_____ Who was he_____

What moment would you re-live:

_____

B-Now if you could go back and change one moment…go back and change something you did or said with a previous partner:

How old would you be_____ Who was he_____

What one moment would you change:

_____

_____

C-Knowing what you know now, if you could go back and change your path in life, perhaps you should have dated so and so or went for the best friend instead…maybe accepted that invite you passed on etc….

How old would you be_____ Who was he_____

What should you have done:

_____

_____

34-I wonder about life and how it would be to experience a totally different century, like if I were born in the days of knights/castles or the wild west. To me life seemed simpler back then. Sure it was hard work, but I believe people were more genuine and open. My friends laugh saying I'd probably still have the tough life and be a serving wench or saloon gal-(nice friends I have!)

Let's ask you, if you could go back and live for one year in a different time-what era would you like to be a part of? What do you think you would have been and why would you want to be in that era?

Era_____ What would you have been_____

Why would you like to see that era?

_____

_____

What do you think your friends would say you'd be back then? _____

35-If time travel was possible and you were being forced into the machine, but you could pick the time period to see: From dinosaurs to the space age that may come one day, what do you think you'd like to glimpse for 24 hours and why? Think hard, could be way in the future or way back.

Time would be _____
Why:

_____

_____

_____

_____

36-That would be fun wouldn't it? Bet you never thought of stuff like that. Would be interesting to see what your friends would say to those, huh? Speaking of friends….

A)
Who's your best male friend right now _____

How long you known him _____

Where'd ya meet _____

What do you like most about him

_____

What is his best physical feature _____

What do you dislike most about him

_____

B)
Who's your best female friend right now _____

How long you known her _____

Where'd ya meet _____

What do you like most about her

_____

What is her best physical feature _____

What do you dislike most about her

_____

How many good friends do you have all together roughly _____

Who are the top 3 you always count on

_____   _____   _____

37-Thinking about your best friends right now, what do you think they'd say is the best thing about you?

Male friend would say: _____

Female friend would say: _____

38-Throughout your life you've met a bunch of people and probably have fond memories of them all, but over your lifespan, the closest people to you the majority of time have been:

Men_____ Women_____

39-I asked some single women to help me out here about thoughts that flit through their mind when they meet someone new. I wonder how many of you are thinking the same. Now I put the scenario that he was hooked up to a lie detector and he didn't know whom the questions were coming from.

  What 10 questions would most women ask a new possible partner? I wrote all the ones they suggested, but you can only choose 10. Now they might not think like you, so I left a space for you to add your own, but remember you only are allowed 10 questions-including any you add….

_____are you full of yourself

_____are you honest always

_____are you demanding

_____do you compare me to other women

_____are you still hooked on a former girlfriend or lover

_____are you a giver or a taker

_____do you fight fair, or do you just want to win

_____do you drink, or do drugs heavily

_____are you really established

_____how many partners you had

_____have you ever thought of cheating…or cheated

_____do you think about your partner when they're not around

_____are you romantic

_____what do you really think about women

_____are you gonna try and control/change me

_____are you overly jealous or possessive

_____is your job going to be# 1 to you

_____are you a momma's boy

_____do you believe in pulling you fair share in the home

_____will you admit when you're wrong

Two of your own:

_____

_____

40-Well, that was another I really have to think about that. Let's have some fun with famous people. If you could meet them face to face, you know people you grew up watching them on TV, the big screen or listening to their music...who would you really like to meet and have a conversation with.

TV Star _____

Movie star_____

Sports star_____

Band_____

Singer_____

Racecar driver_____

Author _____

Scientist _____

Historical figure _____

41-If your friend or a family member got this for you, they must be curious about things. They make the world go round, don't they? So think back on all the good times you've had with this person. If you could plan an outing with them-shopping, movie, go dancing, vacation...whatever you choose, what would it be?

_____

_____

Now if you picked this book up for yourself, you get to choose any person to plan an outing with

Who would it be: _____

What would you plan:

_____

42-How do you live? People have a certain way of keeping their home. Here you'd only be one of the following options so you would say you are: (only pick one)

_____Neat person (everything where it belongs most of the time)

_____Messy person (can never find what I'm looking for)

_____Retentive (don't move that or I'll have a fit)

_____Organized chaos (I know where everything is just don't move the piles)

_____No hope (I give up as long as I find my bed at night)

_____Tidy (I do a regular cleaning and live the rest of the time)

_____Organized (can drop in anytime, its company friendly)

43-And if someone were to drop by unexpectedly, let's find out about how you keep your appearance at home. This is on a regular basis when you're just hanging out. (This time put in the percentage of time you'd find yourself in each option and it must add to 100%)

Can find me in sweat clothes always   _____%

I wear jeans/t-shirt around the house   _____%

I prefer to wear dressier clothes   _____%

I don't like clothes, so I wear as little as possible   _____%

I just grab whatever is clean   _____%

I'm like a soap opera star, high heels and all   _____%

I always look my best, in case someone stops by   _____%

TOTAL=   100 %

In the morning, do you follow the same routine even if you're just hanging around the house? List these in order that you do them #1 for the first thing, and so on.

Brush hair   _____

Brush teeth   _____

Shower   _____

Shave legs/armpits   _____

Put on make up   _____

Get dressed   _____

Take medications/vitamins   _____

Drink coffee   _____

Smoke   _____

Curl/Straighten your hair   _____

Do you always have a plan for the day   _____yes _____no

Like to sit and figure it all out   _____yes _____no

How many times a week do you shower/bathe _____

How many times a day do you brush your teeth _____

How many times do you fuss with your hair _____

44-Routines, I suppose we all have them. Some even have the getting ready to go out routine. When you're planning a night out, how much fussing do ya do? Let's say you have a first date, how much thought goes into getting ready? We women can take a long time for one of those:

How long does it take you to get ready on average _____

How many times do you change clothes _____

Do you take extra care with hair _____yes _____no

What look do you go for usually _____

Do you ever ask a friend about what you're wearing _____yes _____ no

Do you make sure to use perfumes/body sprays _____yes _____no

What brand _____

Do you clean the house _____yes _____no

Do you plan the whole date out _____yes _____no

45-Well you're all ready to go. First dates-Yikes! I would guess some women are anxious and excited, while others may not enjoy the whole process, so on that drive or waiting for the doorbell to ring-do you?

Ever want to cancel at last minute _____yes _____no

Have you ever done that _____yes _____no

Do you get nervous _____yes _____no

Worry about your appearance _____yes _____no

Get tongue tied _____yes _____no

Play out the evening in your head _____yes _____no

Have a getaway plan _____yes _____no

Think about the cost of the night _____yes _____no

Think about the goodnight kiss _____yes _____no

Think of avoiding the goodnight kiss _____ yes _____no

46-First dates for women can be nerve wracking. Ah…the thrill of it all-anticipation, excitement, all the possibilities! So you're finally face to face. Do you notice things about your date right off the bat? What things do you look for? How important are the following when gauging them as a partner? On a scale from 1-10, (1-being yep I care about and watch for it, 10-being, nope don't even notice)…how would you rate these on a first date?

_____Way he's dressed   _____Eye contact

_____Amount he smiles   _____Ease of conversation

_____Talks about work   _____Talks about ex's

_____Asks you questions   _____Shyness

_____Fun level of date   _____Gestures by touching

_____Laughter/humor   _____Serious conversation

_____Amount he drinks   _____Amount he eats

_____Flirting   _____His plan for the date

With the above, there are certain things that we just don't like about a date. So what is your one pet peeve that you just don't appreciate a man doing on that first date?

_____

47-Now some know right away whether they're attracted or not and if there is a future. While some they may take a while to think it all through. How long does it take you to decide whether you want a second date?

I know within _____ minutes/days

48-The rules have changed in dating over the years, some still follow traditional ideals and some hurry. Some don't want to waste time before getting intimate, while others still take their time. Here are some questions for you. At the end of the night, you really like this man and can see a future…what do you prefer to happen? For each, give your opinion of what you really think of the man if he were to:

A simple goodnight (wait for next date to be more forward)-You think that is:

_____

A gentle kiss-You think that is:

_____

A full out passionate kiss-You think that is:

_____

Invites you in for a nightcap-(really just a nightcap to talk more)-You think that is:

_____

Some playful making out (just to stir that desire a bit)-You think that is:

_____

Invited for the night, (ok jump in both feet right off the bat)-You think that is:

_____

Wonder if it makes you feel differently about him afterwards? In these changing times, do you judge by how forward or open he is? _____yes _____no. In your own words, how would your ideal man end a date:

_____

49-Do you have a usual pattern for dating? What do you normally do on the

First date_____

Second date_____

Third date_____

Fourth date_____

When do you normally start thinking of being intimate? _____ hours/days/months or by the _____ date

When do you start thinking about wanting to be exclusive? _____days/months/years or by the _____date

50-Well enough on the dating stuff! Being single, you enjoy a variety of things. Life isn't always about men-you're a busy lady! You probably work, have a social life, activities, work out and a home to maintain. It's not an easy juggling act so what do you do with your free time when you're home?

Favorite thing to do _____

Thing you end up doing most often _____

Do you get together with friends _____

Do you play sports _____

Do you have a hobby if so what _____

How often do you enjoy it _____

What's your favorite weekend thing to do

_____

What is your favorite weeknight, after work thing to do

_____

51-Profound thoughts, moment's when we just think of life with all its trials and tests. We've all gone through trying times, haven't we? Things that just make us stop and see things differently. What is the one thing you learned from it all up until now?

_____

_____

52-Ever wonder about other people? At times, it seems others got it so easy and have it all figured out. At least that's what we think when we look at them. Are you envious of anyone in your life, you know, that you wish your life were more like somebody else's? Whether they're talented, attractive, educated?

Yes _____ No_____

It could be you have a few you envy, so who are they and in one word only for each, describe what you envy and why?

Who_____

Why_____

Who_____

Why_____

Who_____

Why_____

53-Then there's those people ya just shake your head at. You see them every day in life on the drive to work or just out in public. People who just seem to-not get it! The crazy drivers, idiots who walk into busy traffic…it makes ya nuts. What do you hate most when you see it?

_____

Another pet peeve in life! So many things can just rattle our cages at times. We have to take a deep breath, count to ten and let it go.

54-Shopping-now there's a topic. We all have to do it for food, clothes, shoes…so let's ask what's your

Favorite place to shop _____

Favorite thing to shop for _____

Are you a patient shopper _____yes _____no

Will you go from store to store for the best deal _____yes _____no

Do you just run in and pick up what you need _____yes _____no

Do you like to browse _____yes _____no

What do you hate shopping for_____

Do you like shopping with a man _____yes _____no

Who is your favorite person to shop with

Female: _____   Male: _____

Who do you hate shopping with the most _____

55-If you had extra money right now, like an extra $10,000, the bills are all paid so it's extra and you could buy anything you wanted at this very moment. Think on that...is there one big-ticket item or many? What would you buy? (Top 6 please)

_____   _____

_____   _____

_____   _____

56-Since we're talking of money, for a lot of us that is the biggest worry in the world. Never seems we have enough of it. In making our way, we do what we need to make our lives what we wish. How do you feel about your situation financially right now? (You can only pick one here)

_____Doing ok   _____Just making it

_____I'm comfortable   _____Need a second income

_____I don't worry about it   _____Paycheck to Paycheck

_____Geez, I need the lotto to fix this   _____I am wealthy I don't worry

57-The stress of life; work, bills, debt, problems, is there never an end? A friend once said life is not about happiness but about moments that make us happy. He believes we are not supposed to wake up every morning happy, but go through the motions, do what we have to and enjoy those tiny happy moments when they come. Okay so he's different, but I guess it depends on the individual. What do you feel? On each of the following, insert the percentage, you would say describes your feel overall. Now remember…it has to add up to 100 percent. You wake up:

Feeling positive   _____%

Feeling negative   _____%

Just go through the motions   _____%

Look forward to the day   _____%

Dread leaving the bed   _____%

HAS TO TOTAL TO=   100.00 %

So thinking on that, what 5 things make you content and happy in your life right now? It could be the car you drive, family, the night out last week…whatever?

1-_____

2-_____

3-_____

4-_____

5-_____

58-We took classes in school that we may not use every day. Whether history, algebra, etc… If you could have taken a few courses back in school to help you out in real everyday life now, what would you like to have taken a course on? Now these are not real courses, make them up. What do you wish there would have been a few lessons on? Example: For me, is how to fix my own car!

_____

_____

59-Well you've thought a lot while answering these questions. You've probably reflected on many things and where you are in life right now. Looking over the next ten years, what things do you hope to accomplish or change? Top three would be:

1-_____

2-_____

3-_____

60-Back to the romantic stuff! So in your everyday life you see lots of men I'm sure, at work, friends or just people you see repeatedly, so let's see if you're holding back any thoughts: (no names so it's safe)

Do men flirt with you _____yes _____no

Do you flirt with men:____ always ____only when ya mean it _____not at all

Is there one in particular you fantasize about _____yes _____no

Do you want to date one in particular _____yes _____no

Why haven't you asked them out _____scared _____they're married _____ working on it

Is there a friend of yours, that you just are attracted to, but never told him

_____yes _____no

Why not

_____

61-Now those thoughts tend to dive into the sexual, don't they? The experts say we have a fulfilling imagination and we tend to think on the sexual side more often than we let on.

Let's see how you think:

Sex crosses your mind _____times a day

If you could you would like to have sex _____ times per week/month/year

You consider yourself as:

_____high sex drive   _____average sex drive

_____below average   _____you've given up

62-Let's see how you feel about the following. You are usually attracted to what kind of body type-(you find it just so sexy):

_____Extremely thin   _____Thin

_____Average   _____Has a few extra pounds

_____Husky-tall and bulky   _____Big shoulders/arms-bodybuilder

_____Lean muscular-athletic   _____It's the mind that attracts you

Add your own:_____

You are normally attracted to:

_____ Hair color   _____ Eye color   _____ Height

63-Society tries to tell us that we have to look perfect at all times. In all those magazines they always show picture perfect women. Now we've all seen those pictures of famous people caught without the airbrushing and we're kind of shocked, yet happy that they don't walk around looking like that all the time. Do you

_____Wear make-up   _____Don't wear make-up

_____A little is ok   _____I like the wild looks that make up can do

_____Heck, I should be in a magazine

64-Jokes about women who just don't look that great in the morning! I'm sure you have heard them. Men can be so funny, rude or downright arrogant…like they are prince charming in the morning, huh! So gotta ask:

How do you think you look in the morning to a man? I think I am:

_____cuddly and cute

_____oh my god, wish I could disappear

_____like to wake up early and fix up a bit before he's awake

_____I wake up looking like I did before I went to sleep

_____am a goddess, don't care what he thinks

_____hate the way I look, but he thinks I'm cute

Describe your worst morning so far when waking up next to someone for the first time:

_____

_____

65-Now that you've finished laughing at that one, what do you just find so sexy about a man first thing in the morning? Could be the way they're wrapped up next to you or the messy hair, the slow way they move, that boyish sleepy look.

_____

Now the flip side, describe the most unattractive morning you've had so far. When you turn over and see him lying there and you just wanted to kick yourself about it.

_____

_____

66-When do you enjoy sex the most? We all like different times of the day...but when do you feel you are at your best?

_____mornings   _____afternoons   _____just home from work

_____evenings   _____late nights   _____after a night out

67-So let's find out what you've experienced so far

Strangest place you ever had sex was:

_____

Most risqué place you've ever had sex:

_____

Favorite position is _____

Most uncomfortable place was:

_____

Most romantic place was:

_____

Ever experienced any of the following:

Hot oils	_____yes	_____no	_____want to
Toys	_____yes	_____no	_____want to
S & M	_____yes	_____no	_____want to
Role-playing	_____yes	_____no	_____want to
Being tied up	_____yes	_____no	_____want to
Tie someone up	_____yes	_____no	_____want to
Dominance	_____yes	_____no	_____want to
Sensual massage	_____yes	_____no	_____want to

Where would you like to have sex just once?

_____

What would you like to try just once?

_____

68-Fantasies-we all like to think about things, yet we don't talk about them that often. So here it is straight up-What one fantasy would you like to live out?

_____

_____

_____

69-We talked about different areas of attraction already. So let's say you found a man and things are great, so far. You're back at your place or his after a night out and things are definitely moving to the bedroom. What crosses a woman's mind at those first moments? Could be any of the following, but what do you focus on the most? Put the following in order of importance to you. (1 being most important) Remember this is the first time with him…so initial thoughts.

_____The look in his eyes   _____The feel of his skin

_____The way he kisses   _____The way he looks naked

_____The way he tastes   _____His sensuality

_____Vocal reactions   _____Way he touches you

_____Way his body responds   _____His experience/ability level

_____The emotional connection   _____Positions he's into

_____Takes control somewhat   _____Takes guidance

70-Erogenous zones, those little places that just make us go-WOW! Everyone has something different, from a caress up the back, bite on the shoulder, to a tongue on the neck. What is the one thing that a man can do that just makes you crazy?

_____

71-Now of course not all work on everyone and some we just don't like at all, no matter how many other people tell us it's great. What works for one, may not work for another. So what are the things you just don't like someone doing? I gave you a few lines here, just in case ya got a list!

_____

_____

_____

_____

_____

72-Some things just happen by accident or some people are into them and it's too late when ya realize-Yikes! How you feel about these?

Hickeys   _____yes _____no

Scratch marks   _____yes _____no

Bruise's   _____yes _____no

Bite marks   _____yes _____no

With that above list, do you have a habit of leaving any behind? Yes or no ladies:

Hickeys _____
Scratch marks _____
Bruise's _____
Bite marks _____

73-Speaking of marks and such, I wonder if you mind any of the following or maybe you're really into the look of them and find them very sexy on a man. Do you like?

A few tattoos _____yes _____no   Major tattoo's _____yes _____no

Pierced nose _____yes _____no   Pierced brow _____yes _____no

Pierced foreskin   _____yes _____no   Pierced nipples _____yes _____no

Pierced tongue   _____yes _____no   Pierced lip   _____yes _____no

74-Since we're on what you like and don't like, do you prefer a man to dress a certain way? What styles do you find more attractive? Now knowing they all have these types of clothes for different occasions, just rate on a scale from 1-10 (1 being wow I love a man in, and 10 not my thing):

_____Sweats   _____Shorts   _____Jeans   _____T-shirt

_____Muscle shirt   _____Formal suit   _____Uniform   _____Fancy tuxedo

_____Sweaters   _____Dress pants   _____Suit   _____Bathing suit

_____Speedo   _____Boxers   _____Briefs   _____G String

The sexiest man you ever saw was wearing:

_____

75-We asked how you felt about men having markings in question 73 so let's find out about you. Some have multiples so do your best to describe them.

Any tattoo's _____yes _____no _____several _____want one
Where and what are they?

_____

_____

_____

Any body piercings _____yes _____no _____several _____ want one

Where are they

_____

76-You must have a certain style of dressing. Everyone makes a statement through their clothes. Have you ever wanted to try out a different style just for one night? If you could, would you wear any of the following if given the opportunity or to go out one day to an appropriate function?

Power business suit   _____yes _____no

Fancy ball gown (like royalty wears)   _____yes _____no

Leather/lace outfit   _____yes _____no

Costume ball   _____yes _____no

          What would you like to be_____

Biker gear-chaps n all   _____yes _____no

A Merry widow   _____yes _____no

Red carpet dress   _____yes _____no

Cowgirl outfit   _____yes _____no

1800's wear-corset and all   _____yes _____no

77-Well sports, another good topic! Some people just love sports and following their team on the TV or go see them. What are your favorite sports:

To go see live:

_____   _____   _____

To watch on TV:

_____   _____   _____
To play:

_____   _____   _____

Your top 3 teams to cheer for are the:

_____

_____

_____

Do you like to watch/attend games _____yes _____no

You prefer to watch them at: ___ home _____ friend's house _____ sports bar ____live

Best game you every saw was:

_____

The year was:_____

Best game you ever played:

You were _____years old

Sport was:_____

Why was it the best: _____

_____

78-Competitive sports…whether it's a group of friends or league play. Do you:

Participate in one:

_____ yes _____ no _____used to _____not into sports

If yes, do you do so on a regular basis now _____yes _____no

How often do you play _____times a week/month

What is your favorite position to play _____

What position would you like to try _____

What position do you hate playing _____

79-Well if you're not into competitive stuff, do you have a fitness routine? Let's just see how you feel about the following:

Do you work out _____yes _____no _____what's that

I work out at least ____times a _____week _____month _____year

I don't have a routine really, but I'm active _____yes _____no

At this very moment, I could do at least   #_____sit ups
#_____push ups
#_____jumping jacks
#_____pull ups

I could run/jog _____miles _____blocks _____feet

Now you have to remember that regular means at least a couple times a week focused on fitness, so be honest, I enjoy the following on a regular basis:

_____walking	_____running
_____jogging	_____attending a gym
_____biking (stationary or on da road)	_____hiking
_____rock climbing	_____stair climbing
_____treadmill	_____resistance training
_____elliptical trainer	_____aerobics
_____pilates	_____yoga
_____martial arts	_____body building
_____skating	_____walking the dog if you own one
_____surfing	_____swimming
_____skiing (water/downhill/xcountry)	_____organized sport

80-Well now that you've had time to think about it, pick the one that suits you most:

My body is best described as:

_____Venus (I am a goddess, everyone should worship it)

_____Toned (It may not show, but I's solid)

_____Pudgy (yep I got a little bit of baggage, but I'm happy)

_____Muffin Top (a little extra to hold onto)

_____Voluptuous (I like being curvy)

_____Couch potato (I enjoy my relax time…don't worry about it)

_____Average (I'm looking just fine)

_____Thin (skinny girly)

_____Svelte (I could be a model)

_____Proportioned (I got all the right curves in the right places)

_____Body builder (I worked hard for this body)

_____BBW (and darn proud of it)

81-We all know what we're comfortable with. Some know they have to start a routine and some just love how they are. Keep the heart smart they say, so what do you figure:

_____I'm just fine   _____I should do a bit more

_____I do enough already   _____I am planning to start

_____No intention of starting   _____just haven't gotten around to it

82-Habits! That's what they call things that we learn to do. Just seems the good habits are harder to learn and the bad ones well…we just kind of end up with some. We may even have a few: smoking, drinking, swearing, lazy or working too much. What would you say your bad one's are? (top 5 please)

1-_____

2-_____

3-_____

4-_____

5-_____

83-Honesty is a big thing in life and we all appreciate it when we deal with others, but we all have ideas of what honest is. So let's just see how honest you are, shall we?

I tell it like it is no matter what   _____%

I sugar coat at times to avoid things   _____%

I do embellish-makes things more believable   _____%

I never tell a person what I really think   _____%

I am only open about how I feel/think when asked   _____%

I avoid questions by changing the subject   _____%

I am an open book, hold nothing back   _____%

                              TOTAL   100% (it's gotta add up)

On a scale from one to ten, where 1 is top marks in always being honest and 10 would be you tend to fib, you'd rate your honestly level as a: _____

84-Well let's take that one-step further, shall we? Pick the options that would describe how you'd react:

A-Store clerk gives you too much change back you: ____keep it ____give it back

B-Your girlfriend is modeling her new outfit and you hate it:

____tell her outright ____say nothing, let her think it's great

C-You're filling in a questionnaire and they ask your weight:

____tell it like it is   ____fib just a bit   ____leave blank

D-A friend asks you for your advice and you see she is totally at fault for her predicament, you would:

____tell her upfront she's a bonehead   ____dance around and sugar coat it for her.

E-The boss drops by and your place is not tidy, you:

____make excuses for not doing it ____you don't care about its appearance really

F-You find a wallet on the street, no one is around…there is $500.00 cash in it and the contact phone number you

____return it intact immediately

____keep the cash tell them that's how you found it

____take the cash ditch the wallet-not up to you to return it

____hand it in to the authorities

So, overall you would say you are honest on a scale from 1-10: You are a:_____

85-Well those are some interesting things to answer. I wonder how you'd answer these. At times we are in situations where we can choose the high road. Sometimes we do and sometimes we don't, depends on who we are I suppose. So let's ask

A-You pull into parking lot and you and another car both spot the free spot at the same time, you both signal…do you:

____Just move on give them the spot ____Start turning in claiming it as yours

B-A person is walking down the street a block in front of you and suddenly you notice something fall from their pocket. Now you're a block away, do you

_____Run to pick it up and chase after them to let them know

_____Keep walking it's not your loss.

_____Yell at them to get their attention

C-You're in a public washroom just getting ready to leave when in walks this woman who looks quite distraught do you:

_____Inquire if she is ok

_____Say nothing it's none of your business.

_____Sit and listen to her plight

_____Walk out right away cause your too busy to worry about it

D-You're at the local home building store, just got out of your car and are walking towards the building when you see a man struggling to load big sheets of plywood into his truck, do you

_____Grab an end and help him out or,

_____ Let him struggle-he bought em.

_____At least offer to go get help for him from the store

E-You and your friends are at a restaurant and the place is very busy so your waitress is a bit slow in getting your food to you, do you:

_____Wait patiently and enjoy the time with your friends

_____Do you raise a fuss

_____Do you say nothing and just make sure to not tip her

_____Do you walk out and leave

I wonder if your self-opinion changed, my honesty level is a: _____

86-Now we've covered a lot of things so far, haven't we? Let's find out more about who you are. These days we enjoy so many things that women way back didn't for personal grooming. Rate these in order that you would be able to live without. There are 15 items so 1-15 should appear on a line. Now you're going to put a number by each-#1 meaning I will not live without it, to #15 yep I could do without.

_____curling iron	_____flat iron
_____blow dryer	_____make up
_____bubble bath	_____nail polish
_____body lotions	_____pedicure
_____manicure	_____massage
_____salon visits	_____razors (strait blade-yikes!)
_____shampoo/conditioner	_____hair dye/highlights
_____teeth bleaching/veneers	_____waxing
_____laser hair removal	_____bra

87-In this day and age we can do so much to change the way we look. We see it on TV, the stars do it and I'm sure we all have things we'd just like to make life easier. Some get eyeliner permanently tattooed on, some botox, face lifts, you got to wonder...is it worth it? What do you think?

Would you consider having anything altered _____yes _____no.

Do you think that the risk is all worth it _____yes _____no

I would like to have my:

_____

_____

_____

Do you believe it would make your life better _____yes _____no

If you need to lose weight, perhaps you've considered one of the surgeries reducing your stomach or removing part of it

I would like to have: _____

I would like to lose at least: _____lbs

88- We women are interesting creatures. We can multi task so much better than the boys. Plus living in modern times, we do a lot more…there are women race car drivers, women who've flown in space. We rock! We can do anything and still run a house, kids, make that grocery list. But there are upsides and down sides to being single and times we wish we had a man to lend us a hand.

What have you had to learn to do on your own, that you thought a man would always be around to do? (top 3)

_____

_____

_____

89- Thinking on that and all the chores around the house-what one chore do you absolutely hate doing and wish you could pass onto a man:

_____

90- We do it all, don't we? For me I know it doesn't matter what it is-I'll tackle it first, if I really run into problems, yep I'll phone a friend for help. Whether car repairs, building…I think sometimes I just bite off more than I can chew. Let's see if you've experienced the same. Has there been a project you started and had to call a man friend to come help you finish?

What was it _____

Who'd you call _____

Who do you call most often when you need help with physical, mechanical repairs?

Female _____

Male _____

91-A question I've always wondered about and this one even I don't get. When we're out with friends it seems a lot of women travel in packs to the bathroom. (Never could figure that out) I'm independent I suppose…

Do you go to a public washroom alone _____yes _____no

Prefer to go with a girlfriend _____yes _____no

Is it to use something they have usually _____yes _____no

Is it to catch up on what's happening _____yes _____no

Do you automatically go along when a friend asks you to _____yes _____no

92-Ever have one of those moments when you ask-why did I do that? It is something that we just could kick ourselves for. Ever have a date you ask that same question about? Why did I say yes! Seems at times we just weren't thinking right and figured it would turn out way better. Let's look at your odds, shall we? Over the span of your single life…your dating percentages have been:
Now remember, it's gotta add up to 100 percent again!!

_____ % I always have fun with whomever I'm with

_____ % I have picked more winner dates

_____ % I have regretted most of the dates I've been on

_____ % Boring, but I managed

_____ % I just quit dating

 100 % TOTAL

What was the worst date you ever went out on and what made it bad?

_____

_____

_____

93-Fun to figure that all out, isn't it? Seems when you meet a man that strikes your fancy, you get that giddy smiling feeling inside. Some call it butterflies, some call it nervous stomach...but it is something! What two words best describes that feeling when that handsome man calls and asks you out for the first time.

_____   _____

Now thinking on that feeling, the first kiss can be WOW or OH NO... depends on the moment in time. Some like to see it coming, some like when it just happens. For you the best kiss would be described as:

_____

_____

94-Oh, the things that make us think about all the fun of getting to know someone. Now they say there's a honeymoon period, like months that we make sure to look perfect and smiling all the time. So how long is your honeymoon period when ya fuss and bother with it all?

_____weeks/months/years

95-Are you a romantic at heart? Do you hope for a man who just does the cutest things at the best times? Those little moments that you never forget, like post-it notes all over, he sang to you or took you away for a weekend. What has been your best, true romantic moment up until now (no names so it's safe)

_____

_____

_____

96-Now picturing the next man in your life, your perfect date would be:

_____

_____

_____

97-So much to think about-You know who you are and can probably describe yourself in detail. So let's put it in words for the next man who comes along. Kind of a warning label, because we do have some things we just will never change. Whether you snore, are moody when ya first wake up…etc. Think on this one, the top 5 things he should expect from you when you are in a relationship are:

1-_____

2-_____

3-_____

4-_____

5-_____

98-Now that was hard to admit those we aren't perfect, are we? But if the man can deal with those 5 things I guess you can tell him the top 5 great things to expect from dating you. See always the good with the bad, tis how it all works. So top five things you will be or do for him are:

1_____

2_____

3_____

4_____

5_____

99-I do so hope you enjoyed thinking and going over your life, remembering things long forgotten. It's good to stop and just think back on all we are and where we've been. So these last two questions are what you hope for in the next 10 years of your life. Let's ask….

For the next 10 years of my life, I want:

To buy_____

I will work harder at:

_____

_____

And I see myself ten years from now being:

_____

_____

_____

I also want to take more time for me and learn to enjoy:

_____

_____

_____

100-This idea of mine was to bring friends and family closer in life. We all think on a variety of things, but life gets busy and we don't remember to do all those little things we promised ourselves. Whether its finish a project, take that course, listen more, spend more time with loved ones or laugh more. Something always seems to come along to guide us down a different road and we just move on because we're busy.

If you could have any one person fill out a book like this asking who they are inside and out, who would you want to see the answers from the most?

_____

I want you to make a promise to yourself to do just one thing to make your life happier, better, more exciting, more complete. Something realistic! The toughest one of all…for the next year I promise to:

_____

_____

_____

_____

This is something to share, laugh about or question with others. We are who we are and at times we don't know enough about each other. We lead a fast-paced life with no time to think back or ahead. I am hoping you keep this somewhere for friends to look at and laugh with about, a keepsake to look back on who you were at this moment.

LIVE, LAUGH, LOVE, ENJOY….

Wendy Proteau

Blessed with three siblings and parents who supported my hopes, I was raised in a small Canadian town, in an average middle-class family. Single at age forty-something, I'm still figuring life out daily. Being a combination of realist and dreamer, you can only imagine the confusion that goes on internally. Half of me writes a story with 'the happily ever after', the other half, edits the work and keeps it more realistic.

I'd never written more than a grocery list until 2009. It came out of nowhere as I sat at my computer following an idea. The 'Sit N Do Nothing Hamster Series' is my way to bring us all a little closer in this technological world. The workbooks of self-discovery are a way to share tidbits of who we are, in the here and now. Each of the seven volumes, designed for a specific audience, asks the reader about their lives. I have many more ideas to expand the series. This hamster never quits! They are now available via print on demand.

Finding my inner voice, I decided to try my hand at a fiction. 'And When' was written from September 2010–January 2011. Receiving many reviews, the story resonated, often bringing them to tears, laughter, and at times… needing a cold towel.

Taking months to edit the final draft, I began to miss that creative energy and 'Now What' the sequel was started in 2012 and published in 2013. The story continues to place difficult hurdles, forcing the characters to veer from their chosen paths.

My life would be nothing without the people who have touched my soul. Friends, family, co-workers, relatives…have all been there through the good and bad. Everything takes hard work and nothing ever comes easy. Well at least not in my life. I firmly believe that karma plays an important role. It brings us the people we are meant to meet, challenges we have to overcome, lessons we need to learn and dreams we are meant to reach for.

The Sit 'N' Do Nothing Hamster Series

Unlock Your Hamster-Volume One
An introduction to the series

The Single Man Hamster-Volume Two

The Single Woman Hamster-Volume Three

Hamsters Unite-The Relationship-Volume Four
Dating, Married or Living Together

Heart Broke Hamster-Volume Five
For the tough spots of break-up, divorce or loss

The Gotta Have Hamster-Volume Six
Advertising and what you buy into

The Hospital Hamster-Volume Seven
For those in hospital or home recuperating

www.ingramcontent.com/pod-product-compliance
Lightning Source LLC
Chambersburg PA
CBHW081723270326
41933CB00017B/3279